SANCT

C000182823

BY THE SAME AUTHOR

POETRY

A Dream of Maps
A Round House
The Lame Waltzer
Blue Shoes
Cacti
The Bridal Suite
A Smell of Fish
Selected Poems

CHILDREN'S FICTION

The Chinese Dressing Gown
The Snow Vulture
Fox

CHILDREN'S POETRY

The Flying Spring Onion
Fatso in the Red Suit
Up on the Roof: New & Selected Poems

AS EDITOR

Emergency Kit (with Jo Shapcott)
Beyond Bedlam (with Ken Smith)
New Faber Book of Children's Verse

HANDBOOK

Writing Poetry (with John Hartley Williams)

SANCTUARY

Matthew Sweeney

CAPE POETRY

Published by Jonathan Cape 2004

2 4 6 8 10 9 7 5 3

Copyright © Matthew Sweeney 2004

Matthew Sweeney has asserted his right under the Copyright, Designs
and Patents Act 1988 to be identified as the author of this work

This book is sold subject to the condition that it shall not,
by way of trade or otherwise, be lent, resold, hired out,
or otherwise circulated without the publisher's prior
consent in any form of binding or cover other than that
in which it is published and without a similar condition
including this condition being imposed on the
subsequent purchaser

First published in Great Britain in 2004 by
Jonathan Cape
Random House 20 Vauxhall Bridge Road, London SW1V 2SA

Random House Australia (Pty) Limited
20 Alfred Street, Milsons Point, Sydney,
New South Wales 2061, Australia

Random House New Zealand Limited
18 Poland Road, Glenfield,
Auckland 10, New Zealand

Random House South Africa (Pty) Limited
Endulini, 5A Jubilee Road, Parktown, 2193, South Africa

The Random House Group Limited Reg. No. 954009
www.randomhouse.co.uk

A CIP catalogue record for this book
is available from the British Library

ISBN 0-224-07345-1

Papers used by Random House are natural,
recyclable products made from wood grown in sustainable forests;
the manufacturing processes conform to the environmental
regulations of the country of origin.

Typeset by Palimpsest Book Production Limited, Polmont, Stirlingshire
Printed and bound in Great Britain by Biddles Ltd, King's Lynn, Norfolk

to D.

CONTENTS

ACKNOWLEDGEMENTS

Acknowledgements are due to the editors of the following:

Boomerang, *The Gift: New Writing for the NHS* (Stride), *Haiku Quarterly*, *London Magazine*, *London Review of Books*, *Magma*, *New Writing 12*, *The North*, Poetry International (Rotterdam) website, *Poetry London*, *Poetry Review*, *Poetry Wales*, *The Red Wheelbarrow*, *Southword*, *Stand*, *3am Magazine*, *Times Literary Supplement*, *The Wolf*

'Lost' was commissioned by the Ulster Museum and appeared in the anthology *A Conversation Piece* edited by Adrian Rice and Angela Reid (Abbey Press, Magni 2002) – the poem is a response to Daniel O'Neill's painting 'Three Friends'; 'Black Beams' was commissioned for the opening of the Jerwood library at the Trinity College of Music, Greenwich; 'Red, Yellow' was commissioned by the Gulbenkian Foundation; 'A Night in a Mexican Hotel' was commissioned by the BBC for their Proms programme. 'The Dance' is a very oblique response to Paula Rego's painting of the same name.

Some of the poems have previously appeared in the following books: *Up on the Roof* (Faber), *A Picnic on Ice: Selected Poems* (Signal Editions/Vehicule Press), *Where Fishermen Can't Swim* (Bonnefant Press), *Het ijshotel* (Atlas), *No Arroje Piedras a Este Letrero: Poemas Escogidos* (Trilce Editiones), *Picnic pe gheaţă (Editura UVT*/Brumar).

ZERO HOUR

Tomorrow all the trains will stop
and we will be stranded. Cars
have already been immobilised
by the petrol wars, and sit
abandoned, along the roadsides.
The airports, for two days now,
are closed-off zones where dogs
congregate loudly on the runways.

To be in possession of a bicycle
is to risk your life. My neighbour,
a doctor, has somehow acquired a horse
and rides to his practice, a rifle
clearly visible beneath the reins,
I sit in front of the television
for each successive news bulletin
then reach for the whisky bottle.

How long before the shelves are empty
in the supermarkets? The first riots
are raging as I write, and who
out there could have predicted
this sudden countdown to zero hour,
all the paraphernalia of our comfort
stamped obsolete, our memories
fighting to keep us sane and upright?

THE UFO

A UFO landed in Ireland in '54,
in Donegal, in my back garden.
At the controls was my grandfather,
and not wanting his craft to be seen,
he had a house built around it,
or he added bricks to the turfhouse
till his spaceship had a coat
and no earthly visitor could guess
that alien splendour was there.
I was two when it landed
but I can just about remember.
I can hear the noise it made —
a humming that scared me,
as if it might take off again,
scattering bricks everywhere,
taking my grandfather away,
but he walked into the house
and switched the lights on —
no need for paraffin and matches,
just a bulb hanging there
like our own small moon,
and this was repeated in every room,
and a copper kettle boiled
away from the fire,
and my grandfather took me
out to the turfhouse
to see the thing being fed,
but I closed my eyes
stuck my fingers in my ears,
and cried.

LOST

Three days since the boat's come,
the weather worsening by the hour.
Last month it was three weeks –
the helicopter brought medicines,
stale loaves, tins of Spam.

A gull bent-backed in the wind,
getting nowhere. Mundy's bin
tossing on the waves. The electricity wires
taut as fiddle strings, loosing
their own ghostly music.

Where are the crows that sit on them?
And where are the artists to paint all this?
They come like tourists
when the weather's fine, taking
whatever we have.

The last corncrake I saw
went away in a painting.
So did my three-legged dog.
And, after they were painted with me,
my two friends went to the mainland.

What kept me behind?
Well, they sneaked out on me
while I slept off a siege of drink.
They were shits, surely,
but the painting made them that way.

I see the three of us again
on that canvas, the sunlight
only on me. No wonder
they changed. And my eyes
looking nowhere, already lost.

A DREAM OF HONEY

I dreamed that bees were extinct,
had been for decades, and honey
was a fabled memory, except for jars
hoarded by ancient, wealthy gourmets.
Honey was still on the shelves, of course –
that's what they'd named the sweet concoction
chemists had arrived at, and it sold well,
not just to those who knew no better,
and the day was coming fast when no one
alive would be able to taste the difference.

Then one Friday morning in Riga
a peasant woman arrived by horse and cart
at the old Zeppelin Hangars market
and set up her stall with jars of honey
flavoured by the various flowers. Around her
sellers of the new honey gawped, then sniffed
as she screwed the lids off, then glared
as her jars were snapped up in minutes,
and she climbed on her cart again
and let the horse take her away.

In the dream, e-mails sped everywhere
about this resurrection of honey,
and supermarket-suppliers scoured Latvia,
knocking on every door, sending helicopters
low over houses, looking for beehives,
but after a month they gave it up,
and the woman never appeared again
though rumours of her honey-selling
came over the border from Russia
and continued beyond the dream.

RED, YELLOW

I saw from an airship the top of Big Ben
and I dropped a bag of red paint on it.

And I heard and saw the shouting and pointing
as I followed the windy path of the Thames,

all the time waiting for jets to follow me
and shoot me down into the murky water

where corpses can hide out for months,
softening, losing weight, aspiring to bone

but no twitchy uniformed boy was sent.
Did they not care about their Big Ben?

Or was I being accused of being an artist?
The West Wind hurried me towards Belgium.

I stared down at the blue of the sea
which was turquoise from this height.

I wanted to go back and drop that colour
on top of my carefully chosen red

but the West Wind had other ideas,
and was insisting I enter German airspace

although it was southward I wanted to go –
to Italy, where I would be appreciated

when I dropped my bag of yellow paint
on the Tower of Pisa, and watched it slide

in silken patterns of the deepest yellow,
slow rivers of homage to the sun.

SWIM

The skinhead sniggered
as the duck he had just plucked
waddled to the lake.

VERTIGO

High in the pine tree
the old tortoise asked himself
'How did I get here?'

EXILED

They'd blindfolded me, thrown me in a plane
(I knew it was a plane when it lifted off),
flown me somewhere for more than an hour,
then dumped me out and powered away.

I was lying on the ground with hands tied.
I had no idea where I was, or why.
I wondered what my wife would think,
or if I'd ever see her pretty face again.

I struggled to my feet and started walking —
small steps, though. I could be on a cliff.
And gradually I heard the bleating of goats,
then smelt them, felt them brush past me,

as hands undid the blindfold, the rope,
and a young man was standing there, smiling,
speaking a language I didn't recognise.
I thanked him, as he waved me to follow.

BLACK BEAMS

*for the opening of the Jerwood library at the
Trinity College of Music, Greenwich*

Make way for the one-legged sailor
crutching along the corridor
and he's been on the rum again,
and he meets his erstwhile Captain –
stands still, a quick salute.
And how are you today, Sir?
Miss the Perseverance, Sir?
I do, and the sea and all.
And the ports we docked in.
And the dusky, dark-eyed women.
Aye, Sir, I miss 'em all.
But this gaff we've ended up in, Sir,
like a palace, Sir, a palace.
And he's off on his way again,
whistling a tune, and words
come to fill it out, words
about one of those dark-eyed women
and the coast of Malabar,
and his voice is low and cracked
and staggery, but it goes on
till someone shouts, Cut it, Sailor,
some of us are trying to read here,
some of us are trying to sleep here,
and with a final stubborn flourish
the song breaks off, and snores,
rum-fuelled snores take its place.
And above them all, these seamen,
the black beams, and the low roof.

*

Hawksmoor and Wren, come back
to see your palace now.
Look at its new inside –
this library we're celebrating,
tables where beds were,
the original beams overhead
but with a raised, sunlit ceiling –
all is light now, all light –
rows and rows of these tables
stretched across the room
and on them computers, printers,
notebooks, pens, elbows,
the occasional head – but wait,
A coffee, Gentlemen?
Here at the back are soft seats.
Move over, students. Let us sit down.
Carry on with your chatting,
your daydreaming, text-messaging,
your visitors are amused.
And please don't stare at them.
It's rude. Ready, Gentlemen?
Let us glance at some screens –
see this young man composing,
and beside him, a young woman
instant-messaging her lover
who's undressed her,
and is pouring honey on her,
and she's writing This is crazy, but go on!

THE SECRETS OF A CACTUS

The secrets of a cactus
are well-guarded – try breaching
that spiky defence
and an hour with the tweezers
won't stop the stinging.
And when there's eight of them
in this room alone
and six more in the next,
you'd want to get a razor
and shave off the spines,
then dissect the bodies
with a sharp knife,
before examining the entrails.
But no minute scanning
or poking with a skewer
will reveal anything –
might as well scoop out
the flesh and stew it,
and hope that eating it
brings knowledge. No,
the secrets of a cactus
are its to keep. Be happy
with the tiny red flowers
it sometimes conjures for you.

THE BLUE FLOWER

In the heart of the stone
is a flower – a blue flower
tinier than a butterfly's eye,
and the only way to capture it
is to swallow that stone,
then rescue it again
before throwing it at the wall,
the outside wall, while incanting
all the sacred names for cat
in every known language,
and dancing a tortured jig
to no music – only then
will the stone crack open,
so your fingers can enter
and pick the flower, carefully
as handling a cornea, then bring it
to your distant lover
who'll wear it on her forehead,
dead centre, like an extra eye,
one she'll see the future with.

PURPLE ROSES

All she liked were purple roses,
no other colour would do,
and she'd her own black hen
whose eggs were only for her.
And in that magic garden
were two apple trees, one pear
and bushes of gooseberries,
and the sweetest of apricots –
so sweet she eats no apricots now.
And she'd run round that garden,
her hair frizzing behind her,
being closely observed by crows,
talking to any snail she saw,
giving herself commands –
till the voice of her mother
summoned her to the table
where everything tasted good,
and beside her plate, in a vase,
were always two purple roses.
Where can I buy them now?

IN THE DUST

And then in the dust he drew a face,
the face of a woman, and he asked
the man drinking whiskey beside him
if he'd ever seen her, or knew who she was,
all the time staring down at her, as if
this would make her whole. And then,
at the shake of the head, he let his boot
dissolve her into a settling cloud.
He threw another plank on the fire,
drained his glass and filled it again,
watching his dog rise to its feet
and start to growl at the dirt-road
that stretched, empty, to a hilly horizon.
A shiver coincided with the dog's first bark,
that doubled, trebled, became gunfire
that stopped nothing coming, so he stood
to confront it, but not even a wind
brushed his face, no shape formed,
and after the dog went quiet, a hand
helped him sit down and rejoin his glass.

THE SUMMONS

A man is calling
from the opposite bank of the river.
'Come here, come here' he says
in almost a song.

His hair is white
and he's wearing a black suit,
and he's shouting now 'Come here!
They're almost there!'

I look around.
There's no one but him and me,
no bridge either, no boat,
no way across.

Then a crow lands
at my feet and starts cawing,
and the man is roaring
'Get in the water!'

I start to wade in,
the current takes my feet away
but the crow hovers over me
and steers me across.

Somehow I make it
and cling to a tree root –
I listen, but hear nothing
except the man's laugh.

He helps me out,
handing me a hip flask —
'This brandy, and the wind
will towel you dry.'

Then whistling, he leaves
and the wind gets up strong,
and hundreds of crows
darken the sky.

HAIR

Imagine a rain of hair
from all the barber shops in China
falling on the world.
Imagine the first clumps dropping
softly on your face.
Reach up and rub some
between your fingers.
But soon the ground is covered
and hair keeps falling –
and among the loose hair
pigtails, ponytails, wigs.
And now blond northern hair
has joined the black and brown.
Dog hair, too, wool even,
and you're brushing it into piles
but burnt, it stinks to heaven.
Buried, it comes back out
or that's what it looks like
when more covers the graves.
And now you're swallowing some
and it's snarling your guts,
and your eyes are stinging
and it's filling up your nose,
so grab a few handfuls,
better still, cut your own off,
braid it into a rope and strangle
yourself. Then lie there
till the hair dissolves your corpse.

THE DANCE

Full moon, five minutes to midnight,
and my sad fiddle draws them
to the clifftop. They can't resist —
the fairies have bewitched it
and have taught me fairy tunes
that ensnare them. Here they come,
like the rats of Hamelin, but only one
of these will fall into the sea —
the others will survive till next full moon.
First the dance: look how they move,
twirling like dervishes but with eyes dead,
as if they're ghosts. One soon will be.
And the Devil's breeze raises skirts
but the men don't care. And they whirl
so close to the edge, then back again —
for now. And in my house on the hill
they move across my telescope lens
like bacteria in a microscope,
and I laugh, oh how I laugh,
for as soon as I stop my playing
one will stagger towards the edge
then fall. And the cry and splash
will echo for weeks in my brain,
till I take my fiddle out again.

HIDDEN

Ask the sailors about the bar
that's hidden from the harbour.
They'll laugh and direct you
along the south bank to where
the road rises steeply.
You'll walk there quickly,
thirsty from the sun, only to find
the gates of a cemetery.
Of course you'll venture in
to wander down alleys
between graves with photos.
You'll stop at Valery's,
then make for the far end
to gaze at the Mediterranean.
You'll feel like diving in.
Instead, you'll head back
and down into town
to search for those sailors
who'll be long gone –
who'll be in the hidden bar
waiting on you to walk in.

HANDOVER

A monkey with a nine-iron
was guarding the door, and eyes
looked down from an upstairs window.
The monkey was swinging the club
at heads that didn't exist,
or at least weren't there yet.
I leant on the streetlight, cogitating.
I had a package to deliver,
one that would bring me a grand,
and a blackmailer to pay off.
I had travelled 500 kilometres.
The smell of coffee roasting
mingled with the sound of the sea
prodded me into walking –
slowly, though, as in a gunfight.
I should have been carrying a gun.
The monkey saw me, and moved
towards me, brandishing the club.
I held the package up, waving it.
An ear-bursting whistle left the house
and pulled the shrieking monkey back
as if it was on a chain.
The door opened a fraction.
I hurried towards it, watching
the monkey all the time.

PLAT DU JOUR

The donkey lay on the road, dead.
Some crazy drunk in a pick-up truck
had hit it, cursed and driven on.
Two crows flying high over the Massif Central
saw it, cawed, and made for it —
two guided missiles with beaks and feathers.
They were beaten to it by an eagle
and sat on a wire to wait their turn.
The eagle set to his insolent devouring,
flicking the odd glower at the crows
who responded with a staccato burst of caws.
The eagle was as bothered as the donkey was
and the latter's backbone was now showing.
An off-duty soldier came round the corner
on a Harley Davidson, braked screechily,
took a handgun from his side-saddle
and blew the eagle across the road.
Golden feathers fluttered down onto the vines.
The crows watched all this impassively.
When the soldier finished stroking the donkey
and kicked the bike into a tearaway rage,
disappearing into the pine-obscured horizon,
the crows raced each other to the tasty corpse.
The donkey was happy to accommodate them.

GET RID OF THE DOG

Get the dog out of the house.
Get him out of here, at once.
Don't you hear the storm outside
worsening by the minute?
Any second now we'll hear the thunder
rolling in from the Atlantic,
and the arrow of lightning it's fired
will already have split a tree,
and what the next arrow's looking for
is you. So get rid of the dog –
let the lightning have him instead,
you know he draws it to him
even through the roof of the house.
Throw him up on the roof, even –
or better, climb up there with him
(do it quickly, though, or else . . .)
and tether him to the chimney,
then lock the door and the windows,
get under the living-room table
and wait for the howl and the smell.

THE SLEIGH

It should have been black
as it hung like a bat upside down
under the stairs, above the rats
that scurried there. Black
would have suited them better,
and would have complemented the snow
that every year or two
brought it into the daylight,
its blue coat faded in blotches
to bare wood, its runners rusty
until we set it on snow
and watched it leave the rust
in streaks behind, then gather
momentum, move freer and freer,
with one of us on it now,
the dog barking alongside.
It never took us long
to remember the best run,
not in a field but on the road
out of town, a steep slope
round a turn that one day
myself, my brother and cousin Kieran
negotiated to find ourselves
heading straight for a lorry,
unable to stop – nothing for it
but go under, which we did,
and my brother, who was on top,
remembers it to this day.

THE BUOY

It abandoned the sea
and came to our yard
where it took up residence
in the ex-dancehall
we used to play in,
and it soon became the star –
a blind horse we rode on
round and round, pulled
by a pedal jeep, a soft
hardnosed bomb we threw
at each other, an overgrown
lopsided football we
had to kick twice as hard –
oh, the things it put up with –
how it must have missed
bobbing on the waves,
even the worst storms
couldn't have been as bad
as being bounced round
lap after lap, a child's
body weighing it down,
a yapping cocker spaniel
in close pursuit, the blue
rope tugging its nose, shoe-
marks on its orange skin,
the dust of decades
perpetually around it –
what sea god deposited it
on the beach that day
and pointed it towards us?

BOCA DEL RIO

Boca del rio, mouth of the river,
and the boats with faded colours are out,
men with sombreros in them
going nowhere. And look at the pelicans
sitting on spiky branches
of trees sticking out of the water —
one occasionally setting off
on long circling low flights,
coming back with nothing.
And scrawny crows eating lemon skins
thrown away by the restaurants —
and here at the water's edge
a lone vulture, focused as a detective,
hopping up on the concrete boat ramp,
then onto a wall, walking very slowly,
scrutinising every corner,
confident as a diner of his dinner.

RITE OF PASSAGE

Under the stone was a 100 euro note,
and on top was a Scrabble letter M.
And nearby the flag of Italy fluttered
from an oar stuck in the ground.
And a pair of withered yellow roses
was arranged in a sorry cross,
next to the plucked corpse of a crow.
And a red wooden stepladder
led to the sky, which was gravel-grey
and seagull-free. And far off,
beyond the forest, a dog howled
as if it was being branded.
And a single shot rang out and echoed
around the hills, sending crows
in their hundreds into the air.
Their caws swallowed up the slump.
And after the commotion had settled,
and Venus was nailed to the sky,
a fox came slinking to investigate.
It stared into one open eye.

AT DAWN

Walking to the scaffold
he remembered:
the foyer of that hotel,
her smile hiding behind her hair;
the way he held her for ten minutes;
his suggestion they needed a drink
and her agreement;
her fear of the elevator;
his unbuttoning her dress,
then slipping off the rest;
her sudden vampiric eyes,
and everything that followed,
everything . . .;
so when the black hood went on
he was calm,
he wasn't there.

NO

I know no one whose surname begins with X,
and I have never cooked any kind of jellyfish.
Nor have I swallowed the juice of a cactus
or climbed to the top of the tiniest mountain.
No president has invited me to supper,
no sculptor has chiselled me out of stone.
The languages I cannot speak are countless.
I have been shunned in my own home.
I once threw a knife at an aunt of mine,
I holidayed and my white mouse starved.
A succession of doctors have disowned me.
I cauterise my wounds on the sun.

LEAVING TIMIŞOARA
IN THE SNOW

It was like driving through Antarctica,
the road and the fields all the same,
no traffic in either direction,
the minibus cold enough to keep meat in,
and then we passed a lorry on its side,
a car with its hood crumpled like tinfoil,
two horses pulling a man on a sleigh –
eight hours later we got to Ferihegy
where I sat with a Villanyi red wine,
thumbing text messages, playing games.
And, of course, when the phone rang
I got nothing over the flight announcements
except that it might have been my father,
with a terrible piece of news –
why else would he chase me here?
So I called him, asking what's wrong,
surprising him into laughter, making me
hang up, before I even heard him say goodbye.

DAYS OF GERMAN

St Francis didn't speak German
to the robins he fed, nor did Scott
as he trudged through the snow,
but I did as I crossed
the border to Alsace Lorraine
all that winter of '77,
to dine on *choucroute*, stock up
on wine – bootfuls of it –
and bring back ripe *munster*
to stink out the shared fridge
on that final 13th floor
of the *Studenten Wohnheim*,
from whose balcony we saw
far into France, right to the Vosges,
and closer, just beneath us,
the affair being conducted
in the allotments (we rented
the binoculars to students
from other floors), and where,
in July '78,
after the goodbye party
high in the Black Forest,
on the eve of a trip to Italy,
I announced I wasn't going
because I'd dreamed twice
we'd driven off a cliff,
straight into the Adriatic,
and my friend, to my surprise,
hugged me, saying
she'd had the same dream –
and I remembered the first room
they'd offered me was a suicide's.

THE BIRDS

That flat in Maida Vale
backed onto a garden
I walked in once at dawn
in a chemical dream,
hearing each bird singly,
like stereo multiplied,
in all the rooms of my brain —
so separate was each song
I sat on grass to take it in
and fat tears slid down.

And I was fifteen again,
insomniac, giving up at dawn,
pulling back curtains
to hundreds of gulls and crows
massed in the yard below,
hearing the squawks and caws
grow louder as the sun rose,
then, ten years later,
sweeten into this fanfare
no one alive should hear.

SOUTHERN CROSS

The waves reared high in the air
and flung dead jellyfish onto the sand,
while farther down, the hardy nudists
took their chances in the sea.
And yellow-eyed wolf-dogs barked
at lone half-hearted joggers,
ignoring the man teaching the woman
how to play Southern Cross.

And anyone watching from a window
would've seen his hand on her leg –
just momentarily, but there nonetheless –
a hand that was known to that body
that in a couple of days would be brown,
and whose own hand now turned cards
that were face-down on the sand,
being smiled on by the man.

STRONG

Full of strong bitter,
the arm–wrestler stared at
the arm he'd wrenched off.

END

The fat sweating monk's
fingers trembled as he tied
the noose to the beam.

THE MOUNTAINS

Because the sky was blue
after weeks of rain
she headed for the mountains,
taking with her a cactus
and her lucky cat-skull.
All day she drove
with the radio on, stopping
once to pick up a girl
making for her parents,
and once to buy water,
and in the evening, tired,
she fell into a narrow bed
in a small hotel. Sleep
in the mountains is dreamier,
she thought the next morning,
looking out at the pines
marching up the hills,
and behind these, peaks
hidden by clouds. Yes,
she would be all right here.
No one would phone her,
offering work, and no one
would come by. One week
she'd stay here, sleeping,
reading, walking, talking
to any bird she saw, telling
stories to the trees, and then,
before the rain came back,
she'd get in her car and
head for the city of walnuts.

SIEGE

Stay patient, my sweet.
Sit the winter siege out,
watch the sky for gaps of blue
in the cold grey blanket
and remember the summer woods,
the tiny wild raspberries,
the hunted prize mushrooms,
the rumour of bears.
Replay those walks in a rain
that never lasted long –
that path by the river,
the beer-hut, with tables
outside to sit at,
the laughs and the talk,
the old women in black
smiling, and you smiling back,
the dog who barked and was silenced.
And always, after the rain,
the day getting hotter, remember?
So sit at the window
in the darkening light, and smile –
go on, you're good at it.

THE ICE HOTEL

I'm going back to the ice hotel,
this time under a false name
as I need to stay there again.

I'll stand in the entrance hall,
marvelling at this year's design,
loving the way it can't be the same

because ice melts and all here is ice —
the walls, the ceiling, the floor,
the seats in the lobby, the bed.

Not that I lay on naked ice,
but on the skins of reindeers,
piled high, as on a sled.

First, though, I went to the bar —
no beer, only vodka —
and I met my sculptor there,

or I should say, my ice sculptor
whose pieces were on display
in every room in the ice hotel,

and who told me his name was Thor.
We stood in that ice-blue light
swapping whisper after whisper,

drinking vodka after vodka
till we agreed to go to bed,
and neither of us slept that night.

Let me tell you about that bed –
ice pillars, two foot high,
each with a lit candle on top,

and wedged in the middle of each
the four corners of an ice sheet
three, maybe four, inches thick.

On this the pelts were laid,
then the Polar Survival bag
that the two of us climbed inside.

Next morning, over Arctic Char,
he offered me any sculpture
but which could I take home?

And I didn't want to go home
but I went. Now I'm going back –
back to the latest ice hotel

with its blue ice, its silence,
its flickering candlelight,
its sculptures I can claim.

RECONNAISSANCE

From the tangle of a roadmap
the odd familiar name escapes,
cities imagined, even read about,
and a tracing forefinger
follows a road to a border,
over which it and a hand
and a whole body must pass,
which a mind does just now
with less effort than a wind –
call it a reconnaissance trip,
a practice run – and once there
it begins to enjoy itself,
it revels in the company,
takes off its clothes, even,
doesn't want to come back,
but eyes call it back,
ranging over the page,
then the next page, seeing
a whole jigsaw of countries
unfold beneath them,
urging the mind to forget
its journey, and accommodate
all that space, all those people,
but that mind loves the familiar.

HORSE DREAMS

Why does the horse stand there
staring at the horizon?
Is it waiting on some rider
arriving by car from the airport?
Isn't its grass enough for it
and the freedom of the field?

Oblivious to midges and nightfall
it snorts and hoofs the ground,
tail tossing like a flyswat,
but those big sad eyes still focus
on that bend in the road.

Perhaps it dreams of galloping
all the way to the ocean,
and swimming to that country
where a horse is sacrosanct
and can do as it pleases –

can crash through a window
because it likes the look
of the woman selling jewellery,
imagining already her body
hoisted onto its back.

A NIGHT IN A MEXICAN HOTEL

I go to bed in the dark. I get up in the dark.
I lie awake, my head beside the phone.
I practise my useless telepathy
(though once it worked, and it might work again).
I get out and switch the TV on
and turn the Spanish right down low
till the images float there in silence –
images straight out of Buñuel: a plane
flying into a tower, a flash,
then slowly, unbelievably, the same thing twice,
then a dust-ball the size of the moon
squeezing between skyscrapers, chasing
men and women in front – and all this
repeated over and over, like a video backdrop
to a song – and somehow, out of this,
comes your face, and I hear your voice,
freed this time from satellite echo,
quietly infiltrate my head, till I rise,
switch the TV and the light off
and let you have my whole attention
in the warmth of my wasted bed.

WAITING

Been waiting a long time?
Yes, I know. Me too, actually.
But don't even think of getting up
and leaving this waiting room,
this long corridor that twists
over months, over gaps
in the floorboards that twice
you've fallen through
and had to be helped back up
to your place in the queue
that shuffles forward at a pace
of one step daily – but one step,
nevertheless, nearer to that end
you've reached in your mind often.
Here, listen to this music
that means so much to me,
and try this book – I think
you'll love it enough to read
a second time – and maybe
I'll bring a bottle of wine
to share with you, standing
under the portraits of poets
that we might just toast
because they knew about waiting.

AND . . .

And, of course, the road is crooked
and far too long. And no one knows
what'll be there at the end –
a town with a decent restaurant
and a wide main street,
and a hotel to take up residence in
and never move out –
or a mongrel-guarded ruin
where winos stagger up to you,
pawing at your pockets,
and there's no way back.
And add up all the obstacles –
the key for the door, the papers
and photographs, the solid predictions,
the longed-for kitchen, the . . .
oh, just imagine the rest,
and despite this, there's traffic
heading down the road –
slowly, as it's twisty
and rocks are far below.
And the passengers look happy
or are those manic grins?
And there's no sign of road-maps.
And the music they're playing
is rough, but melodic, and a little sad.
And there's looking in mirrors
but little turning round.

NEGATIONS

Style negates soul, you said to me.
I looked at your chic Armani coat,
your purple and blue Von Etzdorf scarf,
and wondered if I still spoke English.
Across the street a white dog barked
at a squawking, one-legged pigeon.
It would die before the day was out
whether or not the dog killed it —
and if the priests at school were right
it was a creature without soul.
It was also a creature without style,
certainly in its final plumage,
but didn't that mean it had a soul
in your mathematical scheme of things?
And weren't you shouting at me
that *you* were the one without soul,
or was this the blatentest of ironies?
And why were you using words like 'soul',
you who espoused the religion of things?
And why 'style', for that matter?
I just smiled and shook my head.
I reminded you about your train.
You kissed me on the cheek and left.
You didn't even glance at the pigeon.

FROG-TAMING

Any fool can learn to catch a frog –
the trick is to do it blindfolded,
lying there, in the wet grass,
listening for the hop and the croak.

And the real trick is to keep it alive,
not strangle it, or squeeze it dead –
that way you can take it home
and tame it, make it your pet.

But early on, keep the cat locked up.
Soon she'll get used to her odd sibling –
meanwhile put a bit of time into
picking a suitable name for a frog.

And research a frog's ideal diet,
also the best sleeping arrangement –
water somewhere nearby, of course,
and plenty of air, plenty of air.

Be sure to play the frog the right music
so it can learn hopping tricks –
ones it can reproduce on the cleared table
when you have dinner guests around,

while you find your blindfold and put it on,
holding your hands out and grasping
the air the frog has just vacated –
making it clear you're deliberately missing.

SANCTUARY

Stay awhile. Don't go just yet.
The sirens are roaming the streets,
the stabbing youths are out in packs,
there's mayhem in the tea-leaves.
You're much better off staying here.
I have a Bordeaux you'll like,
let's open it. (I've a second bottle, too.)
And a goat's cheese to fast for,
also a blue from the Vale of Cashel –
and the source of the bread stays secret.
Was I expecting you to stay?
No, I always eat like this.
Hear that – wasn't it a gunshot?
Come closer, turn the music up.
Maybe we should dim the lights.
Let's clink our glasses to each other
if no better toast comes to mind.
I told you you'd ooh! at the cheese –
here, have some more. A top-up?
You're the kind of girl I like.
Listen, that was definitely a bomb.
Maybe the civil war has started,
the one they've all been promising.
Well, there's nowhere to go now,
so let's kill the lights and retire.

URINE THERAPY

After the needles, the yoga, he turned to urine therapy
so each morning he rose and peed into a pint glass
then downed it in one. At first it was difficult not to gag
but he kept in his head the image of that 120-year-old
Japanese man who ascribed his longevity to drinking his
    pee
every morning since the day of his 21st birthday,
and who came across, on TV, as being fitter than a flea.

And he collected all the writings of John W. Armstrong
who'd developed the therapy in the 1930s
as a way of cleansing the body by reingesting toxins –
an ingenious and impertinent double bluff, he thought
and imagined John W's first tentative sipping
of the warm, newly delivered, deep yellow liquid
behind the securely locked door of his bathroom.

No, he would never let a taste and a smell beat him,
and soon the variants in both led him to nudge
his diet to the bolder peripheries – curries, garlic,
asparagus, of course, the lemongrass and rotted shrimp
of Thailand, sashimi, chilli and basil, cabbage –
and along with the assortment of freshly squeezed juices
he slipped in the odd whisky or brandy night-cap

to give the slightest of frissons to that first sip
the following morning, and bring a smile to the face
behind which all the illnesses he was ruling out
were being listed, and all the extra years he'd live
were being added up, and all the wrong-footed toxins
were unwittingly working so hard for him
before his grapefruit, his coffee, his wholemeal toast and
    jam.

49

THE ANNIVERSARY CHOIR

for my parents

Sing loud, cry out, be of good cheer
for the anniversary is here.
'Which one?' asked a crippled cat.
'The fiftieth, how's that?'

'Fifty? That's nothing,' said the yew tree
stood on the edge of the cemetery.
But the stiff cat shook her head
and a passing snail agreed.

Then a crow came flapping through the sky
and in his harsh voice did say
'Fifty years is quite a while!'
And his beak cracked into a smile.

And out of the ground came a dead dog
who sprouted flesh again and spoke:
'That's as long as I was alive
if you multiplied it by five.'

And the sea itself rumbled a roar
and flung an old boot on the shore –
'It's a gift,' a gull explained,
'It belonged to a friend

who's sadly unable to be here
but if you sit the boot on a chair
his ghost will raise a glass to you
just like the rest of us do.'

And all the other ghosts said aye
and waved invisibly from the sky.
And the moon, who's been walked on,
winked at the hidden sun.

THE RETURN

He's lying there in shallow water,
letting the small waves break on him.
It's taken years to get here.
That dog sniffing his bald skull
can smell nothing of his journey
across the wastes of the sea bed –
the teams of jellyfish helping him,
the obstruction of the crabs,
the curiosity of the haddock.
It got easier when the flesh
was all eaten off his bones,
leaving him sleeker than an eel.
Sunken boats were difficult to
climb over, but he managed it
with the help of dolphins,
and he was not in any hurry.
Treasure chests were no temptation,
nor were cannons a worry.
The other skeletons lay still
but he had to get to land,
and after this much-needed rest,
must learn to stand up again,
then walk to the cemetery
to lie on the grave of his woman.

BOAR

The mistake was having a T-shirt printed
with my family crest. No, the mistake was
being from a family with a family crest.
Do you know yours? I bet you don't,
and I bet you don't know how lucky you are.
And what a dumb family crest to have —
three wild boars! Can you imagine me
walking around with that lot on my front?

I must have worn it all the time
and grown so used to it I hardly noticed
the hair on my arms growing longer and darker.
I began to stink, too, despite the showers
I stood under hourly. And two of my teeth
grew long and out, and started curving.
And I began to stoop and soon couldn't stand.
And what used to be me appeared on the T-shirt

that I'd no use for anymore. In fact, I ate it,
and snorting loudly, ransacked the wardrobe,
eating my Armani suits, all the shirts, trousers
(I loved the jeans), leaving my shit behind,
and sleeping, curled up in the corner.
And that night I dreamed I was a human,
sitting in a Gasthaus, deep in the Black Forest,
eating *Wildschwein Ragout* and swigging beer.

THE TRANSFORMED HOUSE

The turnips that grew on the roof
made a deal with the sun, and grew
so big that one of them won
first prize in the show. The vines
that went from the propped-up door
to the wrecked car made a wine
no one could afford, and the basil
that took the place of the window glass
made better pesto than any in Genoa.
The tomatoes in the one-time kitchen
needed 24-hour guarding, as did
the aubergines in the hall. The melons
that had colonised the sitting-room
sucked all the sugar from the moon.
The chillis in the upstairs toilet
curved towards the garlic in the bathroom,
while the lettuce in the bedroom furled.
And the potatoes in the basement
all had the same shape as the head of
the man who slept in the earth among them.